W9-AHY-525

SECRET LIVES OF
BURROWING BEASTS

SECRET LIVES OF
BURROWING BEASTS

SARA SWAN MILLER

Marshall Cavendish
Benchmark
New York

The author and publisher would like to thank Sidney Horenstein, Geologist and Environmental Educator Emeritus, for his generous assistance in reading the manuscript.

EDITOR: JOYCE STANTON   PUBLISHER: MICHELLE BISSON
ART DIRECTOR: ANAHID HAMPARIAN   SERIES DESIGNER: KRISTEN BRANCH

Photo research by Laurie Platt Winfrey, Carousel Research
Cover: Visuals Unlimited / Ken Catania The Photographs in this book are used by permission and through the courtesy of: *Animals/Animals:* Juan Manuel Renjifo, 10; Mark Stouffer 18; Allen Blake Sheldon, 42. *Peter Arnold:* Rolf Kopfle, 25 bottom; Wildlife, 36. *Corbis:* Frans Lanting, Half title, 22; Nigel Dennis/ Gallo Images, 12; W. Perry Conway, 25 top; David Gray/Reuters, 28; *Minden Pictures:* Neil Bromhall, titlepage; Tim Fitzharris, 16; Pete Oxford, 29. *National Geographic Images:* Hope Ryden 15. *Photo Researchers:* Neil Bromhall, 24; Thomas and Pat Leeson 26 top; Gregory Dimijian, 38; Suzanne Collins, 41. *Photoshot:*; Dave Watts, 27 and back cover; Daniel Heuclin/NHPA, 32. *Visuals Unlimited:* Ken Catania, Cover, 19; Jum Jarvis, 8; Joe McDonald, 30.

Printed in Malaysia (T)
135642

4674

Front cover: A star-nosed mole dares to leave its burrow.

Half-title page: An aardvark, nose to the ground and ears on the alert, carefully emerges from its hole.

Title page: A naked mole rat in Kenya grabs a bite to eat.

Back cover: A wombat mother and baby

CONTENTS

A pair of naked mole rats use their big teeth to carve out a tunnel.

BURROWERS
ARE SPECIAL

MOST OF THE ANIMALS YOU KNOW spend their lives aboveground. We can easily spot them and, if we pay careful attention, learn what they eat, where they make their nests, and how they care for their young. Some animals, though, are not so easily understood. They live secret lives below the ground.

Burrowers are special. They are built to carve out holes and tunnels, where they are safe from predators and can quietly

Its tubelike shape makes this blue caecilian a good burrower.

rear their young. All burrowers have special adaptations for the underground life. Some have bodies shaped like cylinders, which helps them slide through their tunnels. Some have sharp teeth and claws and spadelike feet to help them dig through soil. Many have hidden ears that don't get filled with dirt. Most have small eyes, or eyes covered with skin. They don't need to see in the dark!

Why do some animals live burrowing lives? Burrows provide safety in areas such as open grasslands, where there are few places to hide. Prairie dogs, for example, spend much of their time in burrows. They come out to feed, but they stay close to their burrows in case a predator comes lurking. They can also race for their burrows if a wildfire comes ripping through the grass.

When temperatures get too hot or too cold, burrows offer shelter. Temperatures underground always stay much the same. During cold winter months, an animal can **hibernate** in its burrow. Its heart rate and breathing slow way down, and it lives off stored fat as it sleeps. In places where it is very hot during the day and cool at night, an animal can take advantage of the coolness of its burrow to rest during the day and come out after the blazing sun sets. In places that have long dry seasons or droughts, burrowers can wait it out underground until the rains come again.

Burrows offer many advantages. They are an especially safe place for an animal to build its nest and raise a family. Turn the page and let's learn more about the secret lives of burrowing beasts!

An aardvark peers out from its hole. Huge ears help this burrower sense danger.

MAMMALS
UNDERGROUND

MANY ANIMALS THAT burrow are **mammals**. There are a surprising number of burrowing mammals.

AARDVARKS

An aardvark is a real digging machine. It lives in Africa and gets its strange name from the Dutch people who settled there hundreds of years ago. *Aardvark* means "earth pig." The Dutch thought aardvarks looked like the pigs they were familiar with in Europe, although these animals are not related to pigs at all.

An aardvark is **nocturnal**. It hunts for food at night and sleeps in its burrow most of the day. With its powerful forefeet and thick, strong claws, an aardvark can dig through even hard-packed soil. Like a dog, it digs with its forefeet and pushes the dirt behind it with its hind paws. An aardvark is such a good digger that it can dig faster than two or three men with shovels.

An aardvark is well adapted for underground life. It has a long, narrow snout. A dense mat of hair surrounds its nostrils. The hair acts like a filter and helps keep out dust. Inside the nostrils are thick, fleshy **tentacles**. The tentacles sense odors and help make this burrower an excellent sniffer.

Aardvarks dig for different reasons. To hunt for food, they dig into the nests of ants and the tunnels of termites. For safety, they dig a lot of temporary burrows in their territory. If they hear an enemy approaching, they race for one of

these burrows and duck underground for cover. Finally, they dig a home burrow, where they spend the daylight hours and bear their young. The home burrow usually has several entrances and is very large.

When aardvarks come out at night, they zigzag along, using their excellent sense of smell to sniff out the homes of ants and termites. When they find the nests, they tear them apart and slurp up their prey with their long, sticky tongues. Aardvarks have only a few weak teeth, but they have a pouch in their stomach that grinds up their food. It takes all night and thousands of insects to fill an aardvark's belly.

An American badger makes a rare daytime appearance.

BADGERS

Like an aardvark, a badger is built for burrowing. It has thick fur, tough skin, and a strong body with powerful shoulders. On the tips of its large paws, it has long, thick claws. Badgers can tunnel through very hard soil with amazing speed. There have even been reports of badgers digging through pavement!

Badgers are members of the weasel family and are relatives of minks and otters. There are eight **species** of badgers in the world. The American badger is the only kind that lives in North America.

Badgers spend the day snoozing in their burrows and come out at night to hunt. They live in a variety of habitats, from grasslands to mountains. And they hunt for all kinds of small animals—prairie dogs, rabbits, lizards, birds, even insects—but they especially love ground squirrels. No ground squirrel colony is safe when a badger finds it. The badger digs furiously into the colony's network of tunnels. No matter how long or twisted a tunnel is, it is no match for the badger, which nearly always finds its way to its prey.

The burrows where a badger spends its daytime hours during the summer and fall are fairly simple. They are just temporary places to sleep. But when winter approaches, badgers dig bigger and more complex tunnels. At the end of their main tunnel, they dig out the large chamber that they will use for sleeping. They also dig side tunnels, which they use as toilets. Badgers don't actually hibernate during the

WINTER BADGER BURROWS

A badger's winter home is long and deep. Some burrows have as many as 33 feet (10 meters) of tunnels and are as deep as 10 feet (3 meters) below the surface.

winter. They sleep during the coldest weather, but on milder nights they come out to hunt.

Badgers have an odd way of reproducing. Even though they mate in the early fall, the **embryos** don't begin to grow until around January. When the babies are born in early spring, they are blind, hairless, and helpless. But they grow quickly and soon begin following their mother out into the night to learn the art of hunting. In just a few weeks, they are on their own.

These badger cubs are almost ready to go off hunting.

With their huge forefeet, immense claws, and weird nose tentacles, star-nosed moles are some of the strangest-looking animals on the planet.

STAR-NOSED MOLES

When you think of digging mammals, do you think of moles first? Moles spend almost all their time tunneling in the ground.

Star-nosed moles live in southeastern Canada and the eastern United States as far south as Georgia. They are perfectly adapted for life underground. Their heads are wedge shaped and their noses are narrow and pointed. They have huge forefeet that are turned outward like oars. With these powerful "hands" and large, strong claws, they can tunnel along at quite a clip. They brace themselves with their hind feet and thrust their forefeet alternately into the soil. Every so often, they dig a shaft to the surface and push the soil out of it. We call these mounds of soil "molehills."

Star-nosed moles are adapted for underground tunneling in other ways, too. Their velvety fur lies comfortably in any direction, which makes it easy for them to move both forward and backward in a narrow tunnel. While they have a good sense of hearing, they have no external ears to get in the way as they dig. Their tiny eyes are shaded with fur or skin, making them nearly blind. But the moles don't need strong vision. Instead, they move about and locate their prey with the "star" on their nose. This amazing little pink feature is made up of twenty-two fleshy tentacles. It helps them feel their way around and sense whether something is good to eat. As the moles dig along, they easily snap up the insects and worms that are a favorite part of their diet.

Star-nosed moles usually make their homes near water, burrowing into the muddy soil alongside a brook or in a swamp. Their tunnels often open underwater. Using their powerful oarlike forelegs, the moles make great swimmers. They can spend a lot of time in the water hunting for aquatic insects, worms, and small crustaceans. Their thick fur keeps them warm in the coldest water, even under the ice, so they can **forage** day and night, all year long.

Star-nosed moles stay out of sight most of the time, but in the spring the males leave their tunnels and trek along the surface, searching for females. This is an extra-dangerous time for the males, because they have many enemies. Skunks, owls, hawks, and snakes all like to dine on moles.

A SHORT LIFE

Moles have so many hungry predators that on average they don't live longer than three years.

NAKED MOLE RATS

Mole rats are small rodents that live in Africa and in places around the Mediterranean Sea. If you visited their habitats, you would find it hard to spot them, because they spend

This tiny, big-toothed naked mole rat just fits into its tunnel.

nearly their entire lives underground. But if you did get a chance to see them, you might find one species, the naked mole rat, particularly interesting. It lives in the hot, dry areas of Ethiopia, Somalia, and Kenya. It is a tiny burrowing beast, only about 3 inches (8 centimeters) long and less than 2 ounces (57 grams) in weight. And it is naked. Take a look and all you see is its pink, hairless, wrinkled body. Its eyes are covered with skin. And its front teeth are huge.

Being hairless, blind, and toothy suits the naked mole rat's underground life. It doesn't need fur to keep warm, because the temperature in its tunnel is nearly always about 86 degrees Fahrenheit (30 degrees Celsius). (If the temperature drops, all the naked mole rats in a tunnel simply huddle together for warmth.) Because its skin is so loose, it can turn easily in its narrow tunnel. Being blind is no problem, since it's too dark to see, anyway. Naked mole rats have excellent senses of hearing and smell, and they also have a few long, sensitive hairs on their bodies that help them find their way by touch. They use their huge **incisors** to dig their burrows.

Naked mole rats live together in big colonies. Their burrows are made up of many tunnels, along with a nesting

MANY MOLE RATS

There are about twenty-three kinds of mole rats living their secret lives in parts of Africa, Europe, and Asia.

chamber and toilet chambers. They are the only mammals that have a social system like that of bees and ants. Only one female bears young, like a queen bee. The rest dig the tunnels, help take care of the young, and guard the burrow.

A mother mole rat nurses her large litter.

Naked mole rats work together to dig their tunnels. They work in a line, with the first one digging the soil with its big incisors. It passes the dirt back to the one behind it. That one crawls backward under the line and pushes the soil to the mole rat at the entrance. This mole rat flings the dirt out of the hole. Then the mole rat that was second in line runs over the backs of the others to the front of the line and takes over the digging. Now that's teamwork!

PRAIRIE DOGS

Prairie dogs are very social rodents. They live together in huge underground "towns" in the grasslands of western

North America. Each of these towns is made up of large burrows joined by tunnels. Around the entrances to the burrows, the prairie dogs throw up mounds of earth. The mounds help keep floodwater out of the burrows. More importantly, they make great watchtowers. While some of the prairie dogs are busy outside the burrow foraging for the seeds, roots, and stems of grasses, others sit on top of the mounds, watching for signs of danger. Prairie dogs have many enemies, including coyotes, foxes, bobcats, badgers, hawks, eagles, and snakes. When a

Top: Prairie dogs watch for danger.
Bottom: One sounds the alarm.

prairie dog spots a predator, it sounds the alarm—chirping, wheezing, and flicking its tail. Then all the other prairie dogs dive into the safety of their burrows.

Top: "All clear!"
Bottom: Time to relax!

Just underground from the burrow opening are listening posts. Here some of the prairie dogs wait until they sense that the danger is gone. Then they cautiously poke their heads out. Has the enemy left? Yes! They throw back their heads and let out a wheezy *Yip!* All clear! The others come out of the burrow and get back to work.

Inside a town, prairie dogs live in smaller groups composed of a male, several females, and their young. The members of these small groups really seem to enjoy one another's company. They play together, groom each other, and share food among themselves. Every time they meet one of their own group, they kiss and nuzzle each other. But if a strange prairie dog shows up, they rush at it and chase it away.

A mother wombat cautiously comes out of her burrow, with her baby close beside her.

WOMBATS

Look at the picture of a mother wombat. You might think it looks like a small, cuddly bear. But wombats aren't related to bears at all. They are marsupials, like kangaroos and koalas, which means that the females nurse their young in a pouch.

Wombats live only in Australia and some nearby islands. It's not easy to spot a wombat because these small burrowers spend the hot days in their burrows and come out only in the cool of the evening to feed. They are strict vegetarians and eat native grasses, roots, and even fungi.

IT'S A DANGEROUS LIFE

Because of their many enemies, wombats do not live long in the wild. They have lived as long as twenty-six years in captivity, however. This five-month-old is an orphan and is being raised in a zoo.

Wombats are great burrowers. They have short, strong legs and sharp claws perfect for digging through hard soil. When an enemy makes a sudden attack, a wombat will quickly dig a small burrow—usually no longer than 6 feet (1.8 meters). Wombats also dig longer burrows—from 7 to 16 feet (2 to 5 meters)—which they can run to for safety. Over time, they enlarge some of these burrows, digging out several sleeping chambers and creating several entrances. Each wombat lives alone in its own burrow. Sometimes, though, wombats will go visiting other wombats.

Wombats have a lot of enemies, including eagles, Tasmanian devils, and dingoes. But if a wombat can get into its burrow safely, it is well protected. Its rump is covered with tough, thick skin, which defends it from an enemy's teeth and claws. Sometimes a threatened wombat will even crush its enemy against the roof of the burrow.

A female wombat may give birth at any time of the year, but usually in autumn, which runs from April to June in Australia. She has only one baby at a time. Like a kangaroo, a female wombat has a pouch where her baby nurses and grows until it is ready to come out into the world. Unlike a kangaroo's pouch, however, the wombat's pouch opens to the rear. That makes sense, because it means that the pouch won't get filled with dirt when the mother is digging out her burrow.

A baby wombat peeks out from its pouch.

This woodchuck has found a lettuce bed.

WOODCHUCKS

A woodchuck—also known as a groundhog—never goes far from the safety of its burrow. It will sit upright in the grass near the entrance, enjoying the warm sun and preening its fur with its forefeet. But it is constantly on the lookout for danger. When a woodchuck spots an enemy, it gives a loud, piercing whistle. Then it waddles as fast as its short legs can carry it down into the safety of its burrow.

A woodchuck is one of the few burrowing animals you're likely to see up and about in the daytime. Woodchucks inhabit many parts of North America, especially the northeastern and central regions of the United States. Woodchucks spend most of the day foraging for food. They eat the leaves, flowers, and stems of all kinds of plants, but they are especially fond of clover and alfalfa. They also love garden vegetables, including peas, corn, and beans. If a woodchuck gets into a vegetable garden, watch out!

Woodchucks need to eat a lot to fatten themselves up for their long months of hibernating. By October, a woodchuck is so fat that it can barely waddle along, and its belly drags on the ground. It curls up in its den and goes into a deep hibernation. Its heart rate and body temperature drop way down, and it lives off its stored fat. By the time spring finally comes, the woodchuck is scrawny and very hungry!

Woodchucks dig large burrows using their strong, sharp claws and big incisors. They dig a whole network of tunnels. Little rooms off to the side are used for sleeping and as toilets. Woodchucks line their nesting chamber with soft leaves and always keep it clean.

Baby woodchucks are born in the den in the spring—hairless, pink, and blind. They don't open their eyes until they are four weeks old. But only two weeks later, their mother drives them out, and they are on their own.

A caecilian devours a big worm with its needle-sharp teeth.

AMPHIBIANS
IN HIDING

CAECILIANS

HAVE YOU EVER seen a caecilian? Probably not. Chances are, you have never even heard of a caecilian! Yet, believe it or not, there are 156 species of caecilians living in tropical and subtropical regions around the world. These legless **amphibians** look so much like worms that if you did see one, you would probably think it *was* a worm! Most caecilians are between 5 and 14 inches (13 and 36 centimeters) long, though some species grow much bigger. Running down the length of their bodies are ring-shaped folds called **annuli**, which make them look even more like worms.

Caecilians are perfectly adapted for burrowing. They have thick skulls, pointed snouts, and low-slung jaws. They use their heads like a ram to create tunnels in the moist soil where they live. A large caecilian can dig down as far as 4 feet (1.2 meters).

REALLY BIG

The largest caecilian can grow up to 4 feet (1.2 meters) long!

Caecilians have tiny eyes that are usually covered with skin or bone. Eyes wouldn't do them any good in the dark underground. Instead, they have a pair of tentacles, which protrude from either side of the head. Caecilians use their tentacles to smell and taste in the dark.

As caecilians tunnel along, they gobble up earthworms, along with any insects that they may come across. Some caecilians will eat small frogs and lizards, too. Caecilians are usually safe in their tunnels, but they do have enemies. Snakes, particularly coral snakes, have a taste for caecilian meat. The poison glands in a caecilian's skin don't seem to bother the snakes much.

Most female caecilians give birth to live young, but some lay eggs. These caecilians protect their eggs by curling around the **clutch**. When the **larvae** hatch, though, they are on their own.

Mexican Burrowing Toads

There are more than three hundred species of toads in the world, and some, surprisingly, are burrowers. The Mexican burrowing toad, which lives in southern Texas, Mexico, and Central America, spends most of its life underground. It needs its burrow to help it stay moist, especially during the long dry season.

At the start of this season, the toads use the large spades on the backs of their heels to dig themselves backward into

The bright spots on this Mexican burrowing toad help it to blend in with its surroundings.

the moist soil. Soon each one has built itself a good-size hole, where it will spend the dry months safely snoozing away.

Only when the toads hear the rains beating down do they

SECRET LIVES OF BURROWING BEASTS

wake up. It's almost time to come out. When the rains let up, the toads emerge and mating time begins.

Whooa! Whooa! The males call to the females. Their cries are so loud they can be heard from far away. Some people think they sound like a farmer calling to his mule to make it stop.

After mating, each female lays thousands of eggs in the temporary pools the rainy season has brought. The eggs hatch after only a few days. The tadpoles have to grow quickly, for the pools won't last long. Most of them grow to adulthood in only a month or two. Then, when the dry season comes again, they all burrow into the soil to wait it out.

SCARE ME? SCARE YOU!

A frightened Mexican burrowing toad will inflate its body with air to look bigger. It looks more like a balloon than a toad.

It may look scary, but
a worm lizard has
no venom.

REPTILES
DOWN BELOW

WORM LIZARDS

THERE ARE A FEW **reptiles** that burrow. The little-known worm lizard is one. It is not really a worm. It can be mistaken for a big worm because of the many rings that cover its body. But these are simply scales, arranged like rings. The worm lizard is not a lizard, either. And although it looks like a snake, it is not one. Unlike snakes and lizards, worm lizards don't have distinct heads. Their bodies are one long cylinder from nose to tail. Worm lizards are in their own special group called Amphisbaenia (am-fiss-BEE-nee-uh).

Worm lizards are actually quite common, but people hardly ever see them. These reptiles spend most of their lives underground. They are well adapted for burrowing. Their eyes and ears are covered with scaly skin. On the front of their long, slim bodies, they have a wedge-shaped snout that is very rigid. It makes a great tool for pushing through the sandy soil. Sometimes worm lizards are called shovelnose worm lizards.

WORM LIZARDS AROUND THE WORLD

Worm lizards live in warm, sandy places around the world—from North and South America to Europe, Africa, and Asia.

As worm lizards burrow through the earth, they hunt for termites and other insects. A worm lizard will also eat worms. It looks like a big worm swallowing a small one. The only time you're likely to see worm lizards is after a heavy rain. Then they come to the surface to escape drowning in their soggy burrows.

BLIND SNAKES

It's not hard to guess how these burrowing reptiles got their name. Even though they have eyes, they are nearly blind. All they can see is light and dark. Blind snakes are also known as worm snakes, because they look like dark, shiny earthworms. These small snakes—most are no longer than 12 inches (30.5

A female blind snake guards her newly laid eggs.

A baby snake hatches from its leathery egg.

centimeters)—have a slender body and no obvious neck.

A blind snake spends most of its life burrowing underground. It uses its strong, blunt head to ram through the soil. It uses the small spine on the tip of its tail to help anchor itself as it pushes along. When heavy rains come, the burrows of blind snakes get flooded. That's about the only time they come up to the surface.

Even though they can't see, blind snakes have no trouble hunting the ants they love to eat. A blind snake uses its tongue to pick up the scent of an ant trail by constantly flicking it and pressing it to the **Jacobson's organ** on the roof of its mouth. This organ analyzes odors. With its help, a blind snake can follow the trail of an ant straight to its nest.

One of the strangest blind snakes is the tiny Brahminy blind snake. At less than 6 inches (15 centimeters) long, it is one of the smallest snakes in the world. And, believe it or not, all Brahminy blind snakes are female. They don't need to mate with a male to reproduce. This kind of reproduction is very rare, and it is called **parthenogenesis**, which means "virgin birth." The female snakes lay unfertilized eggs, which hatch into females that are identical to their mother. A truly amazing feat!

Are you surprised to find out how many animals burrow? Keep your eyes peeled, and you may discover even more.

Words to Know

amphibians Cold-blooded vertebrates (animals with backbones) that have moist skin without scales. Amphibians usually live in or near water.

annuli The rings around the bodies of some animals, such as caecilians.

clutch A group of eggs.

embryo An animal that is just starting to grow, before it is born or hatched.

forage To hunt or search for food.

hibernate To spend the winter in an inactive, sleeplike state.

incisors The two top front teeth of most mammals, which are used for cutting.

Jacobson's organ A group of cells in the roof of the mouth of amphibians and reptiles that senses odors.

larvae The young of many invertebrates.

mammals Animals that feed their young on the mother's milk.

nocturnal Active at night. Nocturnal animals spend most of the day sleeping.

parthenogenesis Reproduction by a female that occurs without mating with a male.

reptiles Cold-blooded vertebrates (animals with backbones) that have dry, scaly skin.

species A group of animals or plants that have many characteristics in common. Members of the same species can mate and bear offspring.

tentacles Long, thin body parts on an animal that are used to feel, grasp, smell, and move.

Learning More

BOOKS

Berendes, Mary. *Wombats*. Chanhassen, MN: Childsworld, 1998.

Jarrow, Gail, and Paul Sherman. *The Naked Mole Rat Mystery: Scientific Sleuths at Work*. Minneapolis, MN: Lerner Publications, 1996.

Kalbacken, Joan. *Badgers*. Danbury, CT: Children's Press, 1996.

Patent, Dorothy Hinshaw. *Prairie Dogs*. Boston: Houghton Mifflin, 1999.

Perry, Phyllis J. *Animals under the Ground*. Danbury, CT: Franklin Watts, 2001.

Taylor, Kenny. *Puffins*. Stillwater, MN: Voyageur Press, 1999.

VIDEOS

Audubon's Animal Adventures: Puffin. HBO Studios, 1997.
Underground Animals. DK Vision and Partridge Films, 2000.

INTERNET SITES

Animal Printouts
www.enchantedlearning.com/coloring/Underground.shtml
    Here you can read information on underground animals and print out pictures of them to color.

Underground Animals
http://colegiobiobolivar.edu.co/library/underground_creatures.htm
    This site offers lots of links to other sites featuring underground animals.

Index

Page numbers for illustrations are in boldface

SECRET LIVES OF BURROWING BEASTS

About the Author

SARA SWAN MILLER has written more than sixty books for young people. She has enjoyed working with children all her life, first as a Montessori nursery-school teacher and later as an outdoor environmental educator at the Mohonk Preserve in New Paltz, New York. The best part of her work is helping kids appreciate the beauty of the natural world.